A Year In Flowers

Oxmoor
House.

A YEAR IN FLOWERS

©1997 by Oxmoor House, Inc.

Book Division of Southern Progress Corporation
P.O. Box 2463, Birmingham, AL 35201

Published by Oxmoor House, Inc., and
Leisure Arts, Inc.

All rights reserved. No part of this book may be
reproduced in any form or by any means without
the prior written permission of the publisher,
excepting brief quotations in connection with
reviews written specifically for inclusion in maga-
zines or newspapers.

Library of Congress Catalog Number: 96-72641
ISBN: 0-8487-1294-3

Manufactured in the United States of America
First Printing 1997

We're Here for You!
    We at Oxmoor House are dedicated to serving
you with reliable information that expands your
imagination and enriches your life. We welcome
your comments and suggestions. Please write us at:
    Oxmoor House, Inc.
    Editor, *A Year in Flowers*
    2100 Lakeshore Drive
    Birmingham, AL 35209
To order additional publications, call
1-205-877-6560.

Editor-in-Chief: Nancy Fitzpatrick Wyatt
Editorial Director, Special Interest Publications:
    Ann H. Harvey
Senior Crafts Editor: Susan Ramey Cleveland
Senior Editor, Editorial Services: Olivia Kindig Wells
Art Director: James Boone

A YEAR IN FLOWERS
Editor: Carol Logan Newbill
Editorial Assistant: Cecile Y. Nierodzinski
Copy Editor: Karla Higgs
Senior Designer: Larry Hunter
Designer: Lisa Richter
Illustrator: Kelly Davis
Publishing Systems Administrator: Rick Tucker
Senior Photographer: John O'Hagan
Photo Stylist: Linda Baltzell Wright
Production and Distribution Director: Phillip Lee
Associate Production Managers: Theresa L. Beste,
    Vanessa Richardson
Production Coordinator: Greg Amason
Production Assistant: Faye Bonner

Contents

Dear Quilting Friends,

I teamed up with Oxmoor House illustrator Kelly Davis to design this sampler quilt, which depicts a different flower for each month of the year. Friends of mine and guild sisters Cyndi Wheeler and Ruth Watterson turned our design into a quilt. Cyndi, a master at machine appliqué, sewed all the blocks, and Ruth did the fine hand quilting.

I chose two different fabrics, a print and a solid, to make each of the baskets and set them on a background of tone-on-tone muslin. I chose a bright botanical print for the outer border and the backing, and coordinating prints for the inner border and sashing.

You'll find close-up photography of the blocks along with complete instructions for piecing and appliqué. And when you've completed all your blocks, turn to page 40 for complete instructions and diagrams for finishing your quilt.

Happy stitching,

WORKSHOP

Selecting Fabrics

The best fabric for quilts is 100% cotton. Yardage requirements are based on 44"-wide fabric and allow for shrinkage. All fabrics, including backing, should be machine-washed, dried, and pressed before cutting. Use warm water and detergent but not fabric softener.

Necessary Notions

- Scissors
- Rotary cutter and mat
- Acrylic rulers
- Template plastic
- Pencils for marking cutting lines
- Sewing needles
- Sewing thread
- Sewing machine
- Seam ripper
- Pins
- Iron and ironing board
- Quilting needles
- Thimble
- Hand quilting thread
- Machine quilting thread

Making Templates

A template is a duplication of a printed pattern, made from a sturdy material, which is traced onto fabric. Many regular shapes such as squares and triangles can be marked directly on the fabric with a ruler, but you need templates for other shapes. Some quiltmakers use templates for all shapes.

You can trace patterns directly onto template plastic. Or make a template by tracing a pattern onto graph paper and gluing the paper to posterboard or sandpaper. (Sandpaper will not slip on fabric.)

When a large pattern is given in two pieces, make one template for the complete piece.

Cut out the template on the marked line. It is important that a template be traced, marked, and cut accurately. If desired, punch out corner dots with a ⅛"-diameter hole punch **(Diagram 1).**

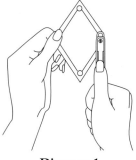

Diagram 1

Mark each template with its letter and grain line. Verify the template's accuracy, placing it over the printed pattern. Any discrepancy, however small, is multiplied many times as the quilt is assembled. Another way to check templates' accuracy is to make a test block before cutting more pieces.

Tracing Templates on Fabric

For hand piecing, templates should be cut to the finished size of the piece so seam lines can be marked on the fabric. Avoiding the selvage, place the template *facedown* on the *wrong* side of the fabric, aligning the template grain line with the straight grain. Hold the template firmly and trace around it. Repeat as needed, leaving ½" between tracings **(Diagram 2).**

Diagram 2

For machine piecing, templates should include seam allowances. These templates are used in the same manner as for hand piecing, but you can mark the fabric using common lines for efficient cutting **(Diagram 3).** Mark corners on fabric through holes in the template.

Diagram 3

For hand or machine piecing, use window templates to enhance accuracy by drawing and cutting out both cutting and sewing lines. The guidance of a drawn seam line is very useful for sewing set-in seams, when pivoting at a precise point is critical. Used on the right side of the fabric, window templates help you cut specific motifs with accuracy **(Diagram 4).**

For hand appliqué, templates should be made the finished size. Place templates *faceup* on the *right* side of the fabric. Position tracings at least ½" apart **(Diagram 5).** Add a ¼" seam allowance around pieces when cutting.

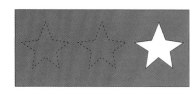

Diagram 4

Diagram 5

Cutting

Grain Lines

Woven threads form the fabric's grain. Lengthwise grain, parallel to the selvages, has the least stretch; crosswise grain has a little more give.

Long strips such as borders should be cut lengthwise whenever possible and cut first to ensure that you have the necessary length. Usually, other pieces can be cut aligned with either grain.

Bias is the 45° diagonal line between the two grain directions. Bias has the most stretch and is used for curving strips such as flower stems. Bias is often preferred for binding.

Never use the selvage (finished edge). Selvage does not react to washing, drying, and pressing like the rest of the fabric and may pucker when the finished quilt is laundered.

Rotary Cutting

A rotary cutter, used with a protective mat and a ruler, takes getting used to but is very efficient for cutting strips, squares, and triangles. A rotary cutter is fast because you can measure and cut multiple layers with a single stroke, without templates or marking. It is also more accurate than cutting with scissors because fabrics remain flat and do not move during cutting.

Because the blade is very sharp, be sure to get a rotary cutter with a safety guard. Keep the guard in the safe position at all times, except when making a cut. *Always keep the cutter out of the reach of children.*

Use the cutter with a self-healing mat. A good mat for cutting strips is at least 23" wide.

1. Squaring the fabric is the first step in accurate cutting. Fold the fabric with selvages aligned. With the yardage to your right, align a small square ruler with the fold near the cut edge. Place a long ruler against the left side of the square **(Diagram 6)**. Keeping the long ruler in place, remove the square. Hold the ruler in place with your left hand as you cut, rolling the cutter *away from you* along the ruler's edge with a steady motion. You can move your left hand along the ruler as you cut, but do not change the position of the ruler. *Keep your fingers away from the ruler's edge when cutting.*

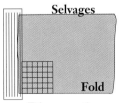

Diagram 6

2. Open the fabric. If the cut was not accurately perpendicular to the fold, the edge will be V-shaped instead of straight **(Diagram 7)**. Correct the cut if necessary.

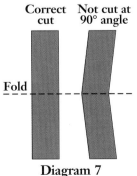

Diagram 7

3. With a transparent ruler, you can measure and cut at the same time. Fold the fabric in half again, aligning the selvages with the fold, making four layers that line up perfectly along the cut edge. Project instructions designate the strip width needed. Position the ruler to measure the correct distance from the edge **(Diagram 8)** and cut. The blade will easily cut through all four layers. Check the strip to be sure the cut is straight. The strip length is the width of the fabric, approximately 43" to 44". Using the ruler again, trim selvages, cutting about ⅜" from each end.

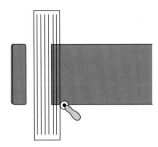

Diagram 8

4. To cut squares and rectangles from a strip, align the desired measurement on the ruler with the strip end and cut across the strip **(Diagram 9)**.

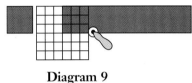

Diagram 9

5. Cut triangles from squares or rectangles. Cutting instructions often direct you to cut a square in half or in quarters diagonally to make right triangles, and this technique can apply to rectangles, too **(Diagram 10)**. The outside edges of the square or rectangle are on the straight of the grain, so triangle sides cut on the diagonal are bias.

Diagram 10

6. Some projects in this book use a time-saving technique called strip piecing. With this method, strips are joined to make a pieced band. Cut across the seams of this band to cut preassembled units **(Diagram 11)**.

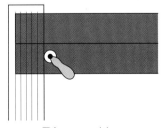

Diagram 11

Machine Piecing

Your sewing machine does not have to be a new, computerized model. A good straight stitch is all that's necessary, but it may be helpful to have a nice satin stitch for appliqué. Clean and oil your machine regularly, use good-quality thread, and replace needles frequently.

1. Patches for machine piecing are cut with the seam allowance included, but the sewing line is not usually marked. Therefore, a way to make a consistent ¼" seam is essential. Some presser feet have a right toe that is ¼" from the needle. Other machines have an adjustable needle that can be set for a ¼" seam. If your machine has neither feature, experiment to find how the fabric must be placed to make a ¼" seam. Mark this position on the presser foot or throat plate.

2. Use a stitch length that makes a strong seam but is not too difficult to remove with a seam ripper. The best setting is usually 10 to 12 stitches per inch.

3. Pin only when really necessary. If a straight seam is less than 4" and does not have to match an adjoining seam, pinning is not necessary.

4. When intersecting seams must align **(Diagram 12)**, match the units with right sides facing and push a pin through both seams at the seam line. Turn the pinned unit to the right side to check the alignment; then pin securely. As you sew, remove each pin just before the needle reaches it.

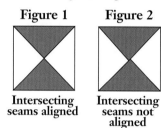

Figure 1   **Figure 2**

Intersecting seams aligned   Intersecting seams not aligned

Diagram 12

5. Block assembly diagrams are used throughout this book to show how pieces should be joined. Make small units first; then join them in rows and continue joining rows to finish the block **(Diagram 13)**. Blocks are joined in the same manner to complete the quilt top.

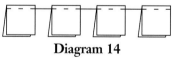

Diagram 13

6. Chain piecing saves time. Stack pieces to be sewn in pairs, with right sides facing. Join the first pair as usual. At the end of the seam, do not backstitch, cut the thread, or lift the presser foot. Just feed in the next pair of pieces—the machine will make a few stitches between pieces before the needle strikes the second piece of fabric. Continue sewing in this way until all pairs are joined. Stack the chain of pieces until you are ready to clip them apart **(Diagram 14)**.

Diagram 14

7. Most seams are sewn straight across, from raw edge to raw edge. Since they will be crossed by other seams, they do not require backstitching to secure them.

8. When piecing diamonds or other angled seams, you may need to make set-in seams. For these, always mark the corner dots (shown on the patterns) on the fabric pieces. Stitch one side, starting at the outside edge and being careful not to sew beyond the dot into the seam allowance **(Diagram 15, Figure A)**. Backstitch. Align the other side of the piece as needed, with right sides facing. Sew from the dot to the outside edge **(Figure B)**.

9. Sewing curved seams requires extra care. First, mark the centers of both the convex (outward) and concave (inward) curves **(Diagram 16)**. Staystitch just inside the seam allowance of both pieces. Clip the concave piece to the stitching **(Figure A)**. With right sides facing and raw edges aligned, pin the two patches together at the center **(Figure B)** and at the left edge **(Figure C)**. Sew from edge to center, stopping frequently to check that the raw edges are aligned. Stop at the center with the needle down. Raise the presser foot and pin the pieces together from the center to the right edge. Lower the foot and continue to sew. Press seam allowances toward the concave curve **(Figure D)**.

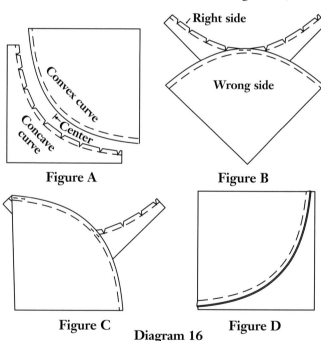

Figure A   **Figure B**

Figure C   **Diagram 16**   **Figure D**

Hand Piecing

Make a running stitch of 8 to 10 stitches per inch along the marked seam line on the wrong side of the fabric. Don't pull the fabric as you sew; let the pieces lie relaxed in your hand. Sew from seam line to seam line, not from edge to edge as in machine piecing.

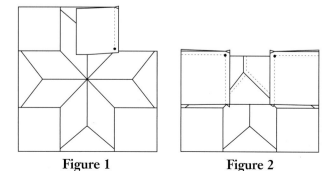

Figure 1   **Figure 2**

Diagram 15

When ending a line of stitching, backstitch over the last stitch and make a loop knot **(Diagram 17)**.

Match seams and points accurately, pinning patches together before piecing. Align match points as described in Step 4 under Machine Piecing.

Diagram 17

When joining units where several seams meet, do not sew over seam allowances; sew *through* them at the match point **(Diagram 18)**. When four or more seams meet, press the seam allowances in the same direction to reduce bulk **(Diagram 19)**.

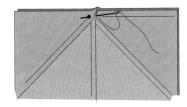

Diagram 18

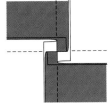

Diagram 19

Pressing

Careful pressing is necessary for precise piecing. Press each seam as you go. Sliding the iron back and forth may push the seam out of shape. Use an up-and-down motion, lifting the iron from spot to spot. Press the seam flat on the wrong side. Open the piece and, on the right side, press both seam allowances to one side (usually toward the darker fabric). Pressing the seam open leaves tiny gaps through which batting may beard.

Appliqué

Traditional Hand Appliqué

Hand appliqué requires that you turn under a seam allowance around the shape to prevent frayed edges.

1. Trace around the template on the right side of the fabric. This line indicates where to turn the seam allowance. Cut each piece approximately ¼" outside the line.

2. For simple shapes, turn the edges by pressing the seam allowance to the back; complex shapes may require basting the seam allowance. Sharp points and strong curves are best appliquéd with freezer paper. Clip curves to make a smooth edge. With practice, you can work without pressing seam allowances, turning edges under with the needle as you sew.

3. Do not turn under any seam allowance that will be covered by another appliqué piece.

4. To stitch, use one strand of cotton-wrapped polyester sewing thread in a color that matches the appliqué. Use a slipstitch, but keep the stitch very small on the surface. Working from right to left (or left to right if you're left-handed), pull the needle through the

base fabric and catch only a few threads on the folded edge of the appliqué. Reinsert the needle into the base fabric, under the top thread on the appliqué edge to keep the thread from tangling **(Diagram 20)**.

5. An alternative to slipstitching is to work a decorative buttonhole stitch around each figure **(Diagram 21)**.

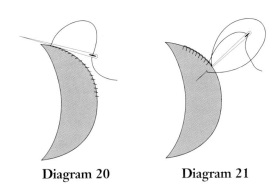

Diagram 20   **Diagram 21**

Freezer Paper Hand Appliqué

Supermarket freezer paper saves time because it eliminates the need for basting seam allowances.

1. Trace the template onto the *dull* side of the freezer paper and cut the paper on the marked line. *Note:* If a design is not symmetrical, turn the template over and trace a mirror image so the fabric piece won't be reversed when you cut it out.

2. Pin the freezer-paper shape, with its *shiny side* up, to the *wrong side* of the fabric. Following the paper shape and adding a scant ¼" seam allowance, cut out the fabric piece. Do not remove pins.

3. Using just the tip of a dry iron, press the seam allowance to the shiny side of the paper. Be careful not to touch the freezer paper with the iron.

4. Appliqué the piece to the background as in traditional appliqué. Trim the fabric from behind the shape, leaving ¼" seam allowances. Separate the freezer paper from the fabric with your fingernail and pull gently to remove it. If you prefer not to trim the background fabric, pull out the freezer paper before you complete stitching.

5. Sharp points require special attention. Turn the point down and press it **(Diagram 22, Figure A)**. Fold the seam allowance on one side over the point and press **(Figure B)**; then fold the other seam allowance over the point and press **(Figure C)**.

Wrong side of fabric   Shiny side of freezer paper

Figure A   **Figure B**   **Figure C**

Diagram 22

6. When pressing curved edges, clip sharp inward curves **(Diagram 23)**. If the shape doesn't curve smoothly, separate the paper from the fabric with your fingernail and try again.

Wrong side of fabric

Clip

Shiny side of freezer paper

Right side of fabric, pressed to freezer paper

Diagram 23

7. Remove the pins when all seam allowances have been pressed to the freezer paper. Position the prepared appliqué right side up on the background fabric. Press to adhere it to the background fabric.

Machine Appliqué

A machine-sewn satin stitch makes a neat edging. For machine appliqué, cut appliqué pieces without adding seam allowances.

Using fusible web to adhere pieces to the background adds a stiff extra layer to the appliqué and is not appropriate for some quilts. It is best used on small pieces, difficult fabrics, or for wall hangings and accessories in which added stiffness is acceptable. The web prevents fraying and shifting during appliqué.

Place tear-away stabilizer under the background fabric behind the appliqué. Machine-stitch the appliqué edges with a satin stitch or close-spaced zigzag **(Diagram 24)**. Test the stitch length and width on a sample first. Use an open-toed presser foot. Remove the stabilizer when appliqué is complete.

Diagram 24

Measuring Borders

Because seams may vary and fabrics may stretch a bit, opposite sides of your assembled quilt top may not be the same measurement. You can (and should) correct this when you add borders.

Measure the length of each side of the quilt. Trim the side border strips to match the *shorter* of the two sides. Join borders to the quilt as described below, easing the longer side of the quilt to fit the border. Join borders to the top and bottom edges in the same manner.

Straight Borders

Side borders are usually added first **(Diagram 25)**. With right sides facing and raw edges aligned, pin the center of one border strip to the center of one side of

Side border **Quilt top** **Side border**

Diagram 25

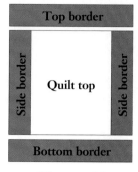

Top border

Side border **Quilt top** **Side border**

Bottom border

Diagram 26

the quilt top. Pin the border to the quilt at each end and then pin along the side as desired. Machine-stitch with the border strip on top. Press the seam allowance toward the border. Trim excess border fabric at each end. In the same manner, add the border to the opposite side and then the top and bottom borders **(Diagram 26)**.

Mitered Borders

1. Measure your quilt sides. Trim the side border strips to fit the shorter side *plus* the width of the border *plus* 2".

2. Center the measurement of the shorter side on one border strip, placing a pin at each end and at the center of the measurement.

3. With right sides facing and raw edges aligned, match the pins on the border strip to the center and corners of the longer side of the quilt. (Border fabric will extend beyond the corners.)

4. Start machine-stitching at the top pin, backstitching to lock the stitches. Continue to sew, easing the quilt between pins. Stop at the last pin and backstitch. Join remaining borders in the same manner. Press seam allowances toward borders.

5. With right sides facing, fold the quilt diagonally, aligning the raw edges of adjacent borders. Pin securely **(Diagram 27)**.

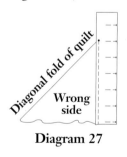

Diagonal fold of quilt

Wrong side

Diagram 27

Diagonal fold of quilt

Wrong side

Diagram 28

6. Align a yardstick or quilter's ruler along the diagonal fold **(Diagram 28)**. Holding the ruler firmly, mark a line from the end of the border seam to the raw edge.

7. Start machine-stitching at the beginning of the marked line, backstitch, and then stitch on the line out to the raw edge.

8. Unfold the quilt to be sure that the corner lies flat. Correct the stitching if necessary. Trim the seam allowance to ¼".

9. Miter the remaining corners in the same manner. Press the corner seams open.

Quilting Without Marking

Some quilts can be quilted in-the-ditch (right along the seam line), outline-quilted (¼" from the seam line), or echo-quilted (lines of quilting rippling outward from the design like waves on a pond). These methods can be used without any marking at all. If you are machine quilting, simply use the edge of your presser foot and the seam line as a guide. If you are hand quilting, by the time you have pieced a quilt top, your eye will be practiced enough for you to produce straight, even quilting without the guidance of marked lines.

Marking Quilting Designs

Many quilters like to mark the entire top at one time, a practice that requires long-lasting markings. The most common tool for this purpose is a sharp **pencil**. However, most pencils are made with an oil-based graphite lead, which often will not wash out completely. Look for a high-quality artist's pencil marked "2H" or higher (the higher the number, the harder the lead, and the lighter the line it will make). Sharpen the pencil frequently to keep the line on the fabric thin and light. Or try a mechanical pencil with a 0.5-mm lead. It will maintain a fine line without sharpening.

While you are in the art supply store, get a **white plastic eraser** (brand name Magic Rub). This eraser, used by professional drafters and artists, will cleanly remove the carbon smudges left by pencil lead without fraying the fabric or leaving eraser crumbs.

Water- and **air-soluble marking pens** are convenient, but controversial, marking tools. Some quilters have found that the marks reappear, often up to several years later, while others have no problems with them.

Be sure to test these pens on each fabric you plan to mark and *follow package directions exactly.* Because the inks can be permanently set by heat, be very careful with a marked quilt. Do not leave it in your car on a hot day and never touch it with an iron until the marks have been removed. Plan to complete the quilting within a year after marking it with a water-soluble pen.

Air-soluble pens are best for marking small sections at a time. The marks disappear within 24 to 48 hours, but the ink remains in the fabric until it is washed. After the quilt is completed and before it is used, rinse it twice in clear, cool water, using no soap, detergent, or bleach. Let the quilt air-dry.

For dark fabrics, the cleanest marker you can use is a thin sliver of pure, white **soap**. Choose a soap that contains no creams, deodorants, dyes, or perfumes; these added ingredients may leave a residue on the fabric.

Other marking tools include **colored pencils** made specifically for marking fabric and **tailor's chalk** (available in powdered, stick, and traditional cake form). When using chalk, mark small sections of the quilt at a time because the chalk rubs off easily.

Quilting Stencils

Quilting patterns can be purchased as precut stencils. Simply lay these on your quilt top and mark the design through the cutout areas.

To make your own stencil of a printed quilting pattern, such as the one below, use a permanent marker to trace the design onto a blank sheet of template plastic. Then use a craft knife to cut out the design.

Quilting Stencil Pattern

Making a Quilt Backing

Some fabric and quilt shops sell 90" and 108" widths of 100% cotton fabric that are very practical for quilt backing. However, the instructions in this book always give backing yardage based on 44"-wide fabric.

When using 44"-wide fabric, all quilts wider than 41" will require a pieced backing. For quilts 41" to 80" wide, you will need an amount of fabric equal to two times the desired *length* of the unfinished backing. (The unfinished backing should be at least 3" larger on all sides than the quilt top.)

The simplest method of making a backing is to cut the fabric in half widthwise (**Diagram 29**), and then sew the two panels together lengthwise. This results in a backing with a vertical center seam. Press the seam allowances to one side.

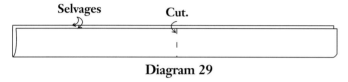

Diagram 29

Another method of seaming the backing results in two vertical seams and a center panel of fabric. This method is often preferred by quilt show judges. Begin by cutting the fabric in half widthwise. Open the two lengths and stack them, with right sides facing and selvages aligned. Stitch along *both* selvage edges to create a tube of fabric (**Diagram 30**). Cut down the center of the top layer of fabric only and open the fabric flat (**Diagram 31**). Press seam allowances to one side.

If the quilt is wider than 80", it is more economical to cut the fabric into three lengths that are the desired width of the backing. Join the three lengths so that the seams are horizontal to the quilt, rather than vertical. For this method, you'll need an amount of fabric equal to three times the *width* of the unfinished backing.

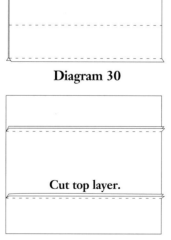

Diagram 30

Diagram 31

Fabric requirements in this book reflect the most economical method of seaming the backing fabric.

Layering and Basting

After the quilt top and backing are made, the next steps are layering and basting in preparation for quilting.

Prepare a large working surface to spread out the quilt—a large table, two tables pushed together, or the floor. Place the backing on the working surface wrong side up. Unfold the batting and place it on top of the backing, smoothing away any wrinkles or lumps.

Lay the quilt top wrong side down on top of the batting and backing. Make sure the edges of the backing and quilt top are parallel.

Knot a long strand of sewing thread and use a long (darning) needle for basting. Begin basting in the center of the quilt and baste out toward the edges. The basting stitches should cover an ample amount of the quilt so that the layers do not shift during quilting.

Machine quilters use nickel-plated safety pins for basting so there will be no basting threads to get caught on the presser foot. Safety pins, spaced approximately 4" apart, can be used by hand quilters, too.

Hand Quilting

Hand-quilted stitches should be evenly spaced, with the spaces between stitches about the same length as the stitches themselves. The *number* of stitches per inch is less important than the *uniformity* of the stitching. Don't worry if you take only five or six stitches per inch; just be consistent throughout the project.

Machine Quilting

For machine quilting, the backing and batting should be 3" larger all around than the quilt top, because the quilting process pushes the quilt top fabric outward. After quilting, trim the backing and batting to the same size as the quilt top.

Thread your bobbin with good-quality sewing thread (not quilting thread) in a color to match the backing. Use a top thread color to match the quilt top or use invisible nylon thread.

An even-feed or walking foot will feed all the quilt's layers through the machine at the same speed. It is possible to machine-quilt without this foot (by experimenting with tension and presser foot pressure), but it will be much easier *with* it. If you do not have this foot, get one from your sewing machine dealer.

Straight-Grain Binding

1. Mark the fabric in horizontal lines the width of the binding **(Diagram 32).**

A	↕ width of binding	
B		A
C		B
D		C
E		D
F		E
		F

Diagram 32

2. With right sides facing, fold the fabric in half, offsetting drawn lines by matching letters and raw edges **(Diagram 33).** Stitch a ¼" seam.

3. Cut the binding in a continuous strip, starting with one end and following the marked lines around the tube. Press the strip in half lengthwise.

Diagram 33

Continuous Bias Binding

This technique can be used to make continuous bias for appliqué as well as for binding.

1. Cut a square of fabric in half diagonally to form two triangles. With right sides facing, join the triangles **(Diagram 34).** Press the seam allowance open.

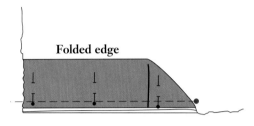

Diagram 34

2. Mark parallel lines the desired width of the binding **(Diagram 35),** taking care not to stretch the bias. With right sides facing, align the raw edges (indicated as Seam 2). As you align the edges, offset one Seam 2 point past its natural matching point by one line. Stitch the seam; then press the seam allowance open.

Diagram 35

3. Cut the binding in a continuous strip, starting with the protruding point and following the marked lines around the tube **(Diagram 36).** Press the strip in half lengthwise.

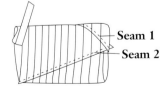

Diagram 36

Applying Binding

Binding is applied to the front of the quilt first. You may begin anywhere on the edge of the quilt except at the corner.

1. Matching raw edges, lay the binding on the quilt. Fold down the top corner of the binding at a 45° angle, align the raw edges, and pin **(Diagram 37).**

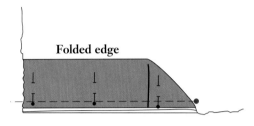

Folded edge

Diagram 37

2. Beginning at the folded end, machine-stitch the binding to the quilt. Stop stitching ¼" from the corner and backstitch. Fold the binding strip diagonally away from the quilt, making a 45° angle **(Diagram 38).**

3. Fold the binding strip straight down along the next side to be stitched, creating a pleat in the corner. Position the needle at the ¼" seam line of the new side **(Diagram 39).** Make a few stitches, backstitch, and then stitch the seam. Continue until all corners and sides are done. Overlap the end of the binding strip over the beginning fold and stitch about 2" beyond it. Trim any excess binding.

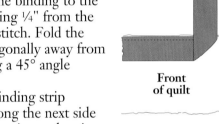

Front of quilt

Diagram 38

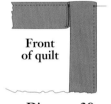

Front of quilt

Machine stitching begins here.

Diagram 39

4. Turn the binding over the raw edge of the quilt. Slipstitch it in place on the back, using thread that matches the binding. The fold at the beginning of the binding strip will create a neat, angled edge when it is folded to the back.

5. At each corner, fold the binding to form a miter **(Diagram 40).** Hand-stitch the miters closed if desired.

Back of quilt

Diagram 40

A Year in Flowers

Your fabric stash might be a good place to start looking for fabrics for this quilt, since only small amounts are needed for each basket flower. But if you prefer to buy all new fabric, I suggest you start with a large floral print for the outer border, then match all the others to that.

Finished Quilt Size
60" x 75"

Number of Blocks and Finished Size

12 blocks	12" x 12"

Fabric Requirements

White-on-white print	1½ yards
Green print	1¼ yards
Gold print	⅜ yard
Red print	½ yard
Pink floral 1	2¼ yards
Basket color 1*	12 (14") squares
Basket color 2**	12 (10") squares
Flowers, foliage, stems scraps (see below)	
Backing	3¾ yards

*If you choose to make all baskets the same color, buy 1½ yards.

**Basket color 2 should coordinate with Basket color 1. If all baskets are the same color, buy 1 yard.

Quilt designed by Kelly Davis and Susan Ramey Cleveland.
Quilt made by Ruth Watterson and Cynthia Moody Wheeler.
Birmingham, Alabama

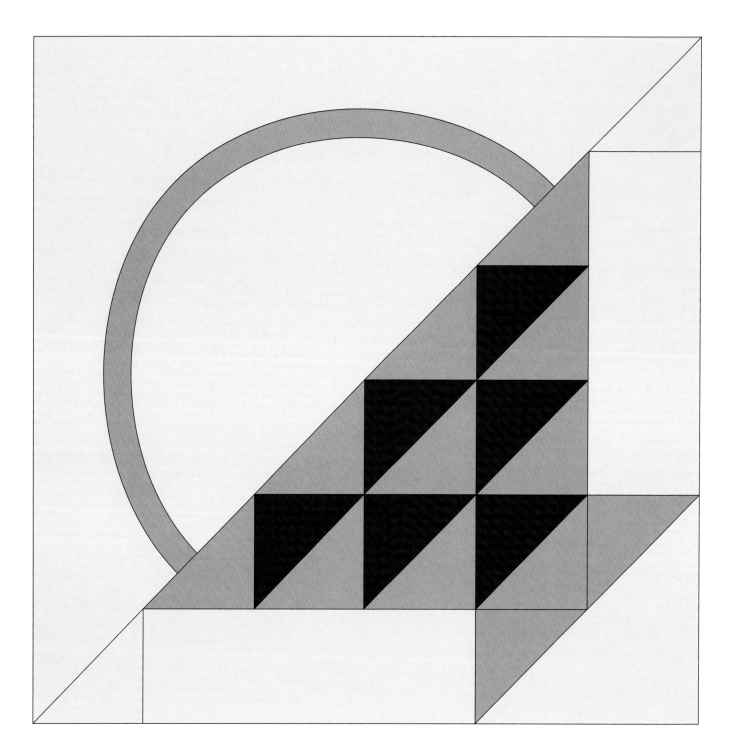

Basket Block Diagram

Piece the basic basket block for each month's flower.

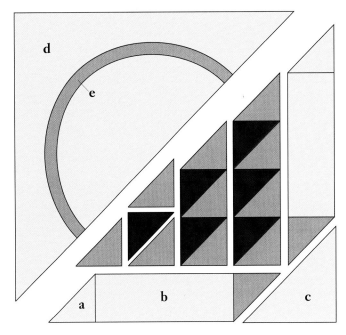

Block Assembly Diagram

Block Assembly

1. For basket handle (e), fold under ¼" on each long edge of 1" x 15" bias strip from basket color 1. Press.

2. Center handle over triangle (d) as shown in **Block Assembly Diagram.** Appliqué handle to triangle.

3. Referring to **Block Assembly Diagram,** join 2 white-on-white triangles (a), 12 basket color 1 triangles (a), 6 basket color 2 triangles (a), 2 rectangles (b), 1 triangle (c), and 1 appliquéd triangle (d) as shown to make 1 basket block.

4. Repeat to make 12 basket blocks.

January
Carnation

Many of us first became familiar with this floral beauty
when we received our first corsage in high school.

Number to Cut

Template A	1 pink print
Template B	1 pink print
Template C	1 pink print
Template D	1 pink print
Template E	1 green print
Template F	1 green print

Note: For machine appliqué, cut fabric pieces finished size along solid (sewing) lines; do not add seam allowance. For hand appliqué, add ⅛" seam allowance to fabric pieces.

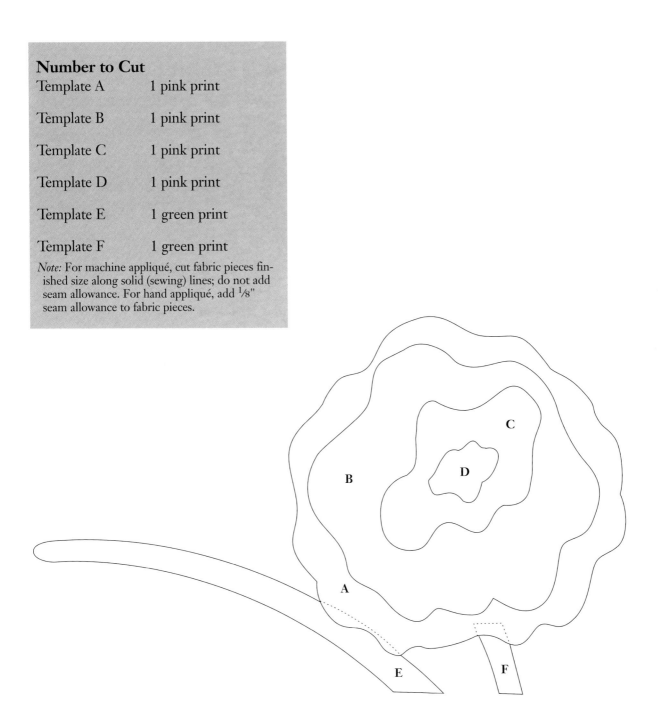

Placement Guide: Carnation

February
Violet

This sentimental little favorite is native to South
America but loved throughout the world.

Number to Cut

Template G   15 purple print

Template H   3 yellow solid

Note: For machine appliqué, cut fabric pieces finished size along solid (sewing) lines; do not add seam allowance. For hand appliqué, add $1/8$" seam allowance to fabric pieces.

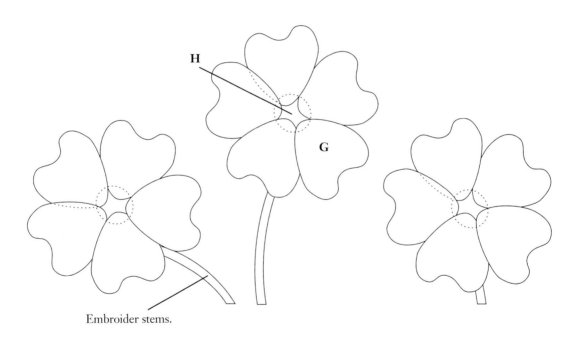

Embroider stems.

Placement Guide: Violet

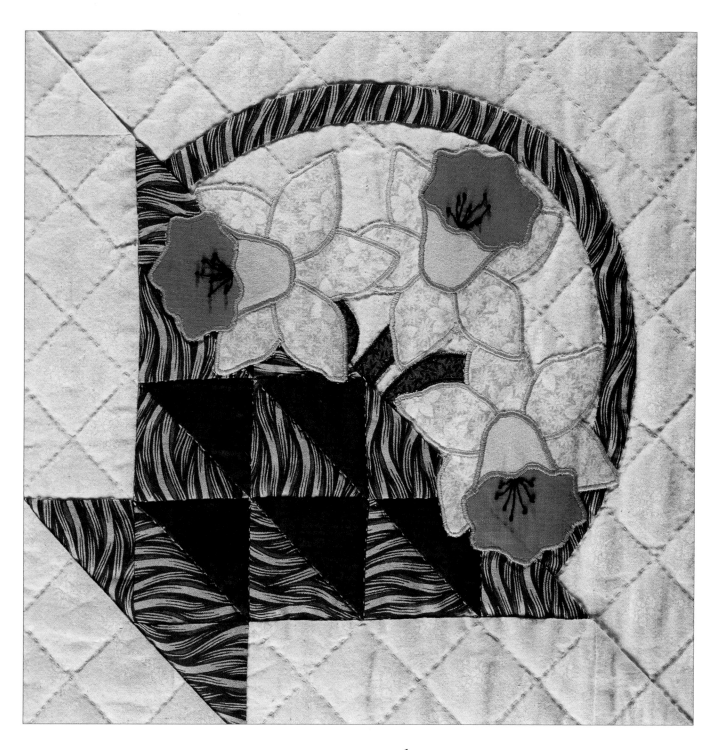

March
Daffodil

These trumpet-shaped blossoms are renowned
throughout the country as harbingers of spring.

Number to Cut

Template I	3 light yellow print
Template J solid	3 medium yellow
Template K	3 orange solid
Template L	1 green print
Template M	1 green print
Template N	1 green print

Note: For machine appliqué, cut fabric pieces finished size along solid (sewing) lines; do not add seam allowance. For hand appliqué, add ⅛" seam allowance to fabric pieces.

Embroider details.

Placement Guide: Daffodil

April
Daisy

Many a young man has won over the girl of his dreams by giving her a bouquet of these feminine favorites.

Number to Cut

Template O	2 brown solid
Template P	9 white print
Template Q	9 white print
Template R	1 green print
Template S	1 green print

Note: For machine appliqué, cut fabric pieces finished size along solid (sewing) lines; do not add seam allowance. For hand appliqué, add $1/8$" seam allowance to fabric pieces.

Placement Guide: Daisy

May
Lily of the Valley

This dainty flower has adorned brides' bouquets for generations.

Number to Cut

Template T	5 white print
Template U	1 green print
Template V	1 white print
Template W	1 green print
Template X	2 green print
Template Y	2 green print
Template Z	1 green print

Note: For machine appliqué, cut fabric pieces finished size along solid (sewing) lines; do not add seam allowance. For hand appliqué, add ⅛" seam allowance to fabric pieces.

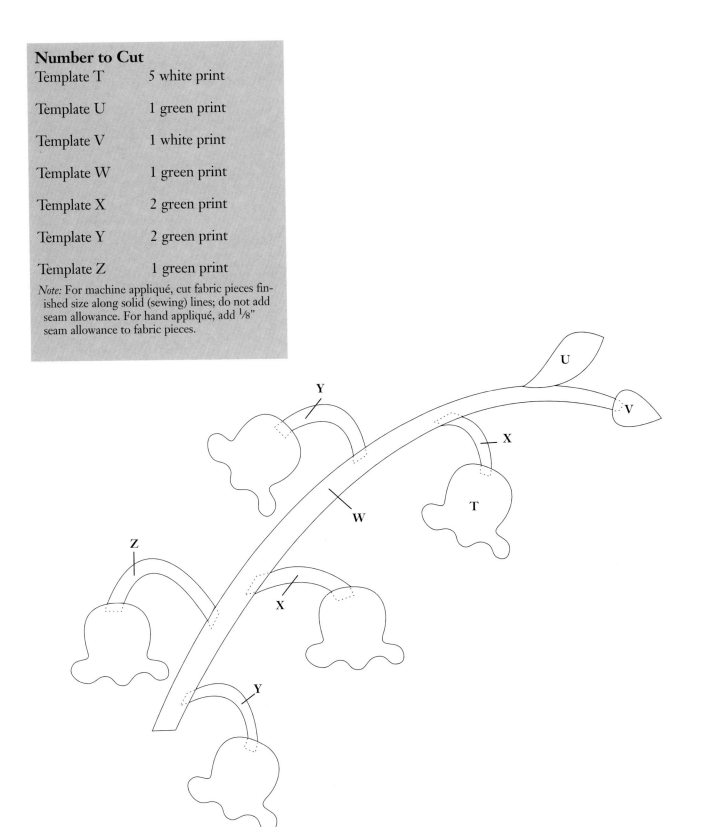

Placement Guide: Lily of the Valley

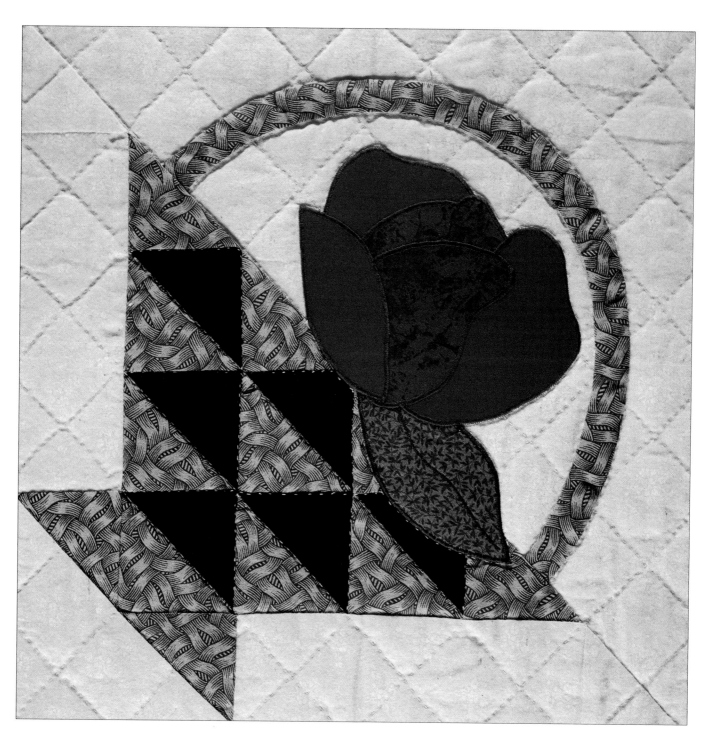

June
Rose

The subject of myth, poetry, and song, the rose is the
most romantic of all flowers.

Number to Cut

Template AA	1 red solid
Template BB	1 green print
Template CC	1 red solid
Template DD	1 red print
Template EE	1 red print
Template FF	1 red print
Template GG	1 red solid

Note: For machine appliqué, cut fabric pieces finished size along solid (sewing) lines; do not add seam allowance. For hand appliqué, add $\frac{1}{8}$" seam allowance to fabric pieces.

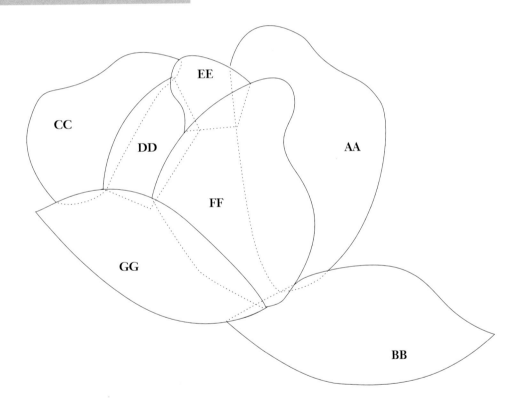

Placement Guide: Rose

July
Larkspur

Though the blooming season is brief, the larkspur's
shades of blue, pink, and white are long remembered
after their splendor fades.

Number to Cut

Template HH   12 medium blue
print
8 light blue print

Template II   1 green print

Note: For machine appliqué, cut fabric pieces finished size along solid (sewing) lines; do not add seam allowance. For hand appliqué, add $1/8$" seam allowance to fabric pieces.

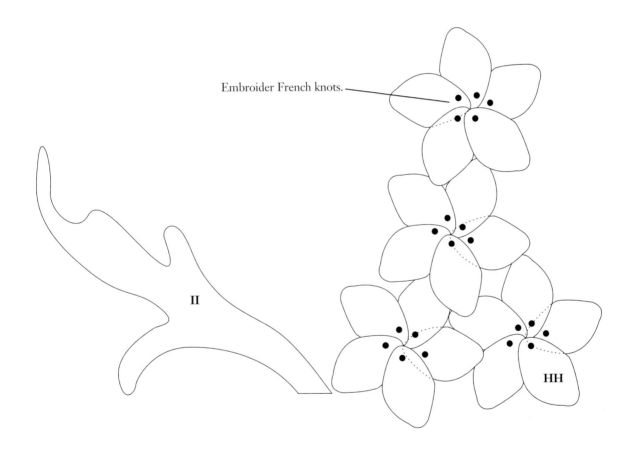

Embroider French knots.

II

HH

Placement Guide: Larkspur

August
Gladiolus

These magnificent flowers put on a spectacular
display of color in Southern summer gardens.

Number to Cut

Template JJ   1 pink solid
1 light pink print
2 medium pink print

Template KK   1 medium pink print
2 light pink print

Template LL   1 light pink print
2 pink solid

Template MM   1 green print

Template NN   1 green print

Note: For machine appliqué, cut fabric pieces finished size along solid (sewing) lines; do not add seam allowance. For hand appliqué, add 1/8" seam allowance to fabric pieces.

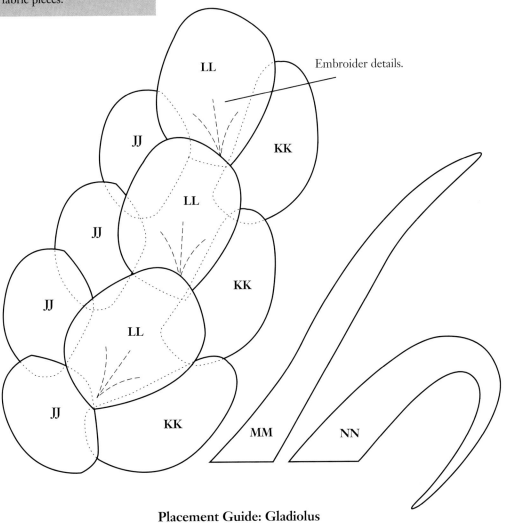

Embroider details.

Placement Guide: Gladiolus

September
Morning Glory

Often seen covering fences and trellises, this plant is
so named because its flowers open only in the morning
unless the day is cloudy.

Number to Cut

Template OO	2 blue print
Template PP	2 light blue solid
Template QQ	2 blue print
Template RR	1 green print
Template SS	1 light blue solid
Template TT	1 blue print
Template UU	1 blue print
Template VV	1 blue print
Template WW	1 blue print
Template XX	1 blue print

Note: For machine appliqué, cut fabric pieces finished size along solid (sewing) lines; do not add seam allowance. For hand appliqué, add ⅛" seam allowance to fabric pieces.

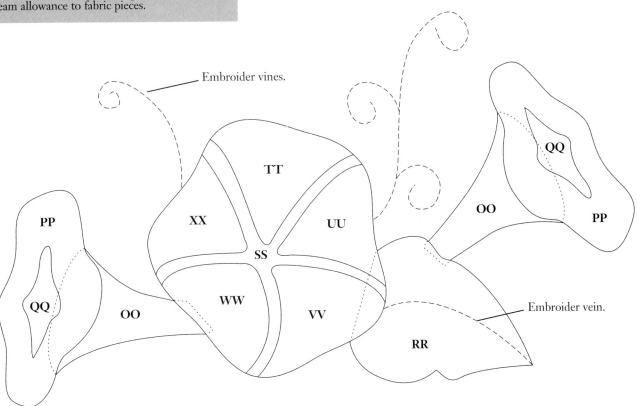

Embroider vines.

Embroider vein.

Placement Guide: Morning Glory

October
Calendula

Also known as the pot marigold, the calendula's
flowering slows in summer's heat and resumes in
autumn in colors of yellow, orange, and apricot.

Number to Cut

Template YY 1 coral print

Template ZZ 1 red print

Template AAA 2 coral print

Template BBB 2 red print

Template CCC 1 green print

Template DDD 1 green print

Template EEE 1 green print

Note: For machine appliqué, cut fabric pieces
  finished size along solid (sewing) lines; do not
  add seam allowance. For hand appliqué, add ⅛"
  seam allowance to fabric pieces.

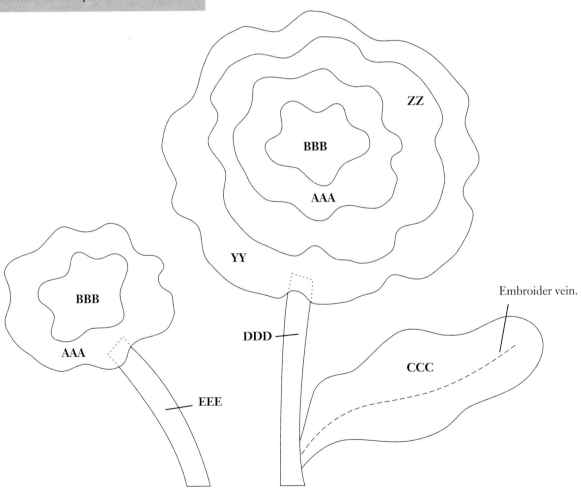

Placement Guide: Calendula

November
Chrysanthemum

This popular cut flower is also favored as a potted
plant in the autumn months.

Number to Cut

Template FFF	1 green print
Template GGG	1 white print
Template HHH	1 white print
Template III	1 white print
Template JJJ	1 green print

Note: For machine appliqué, cut fabric pieces finished size along solid (sewing) lines; do not add seam allowance. For hand appliqué, add ⅛" seam allowance to fabric pieces.

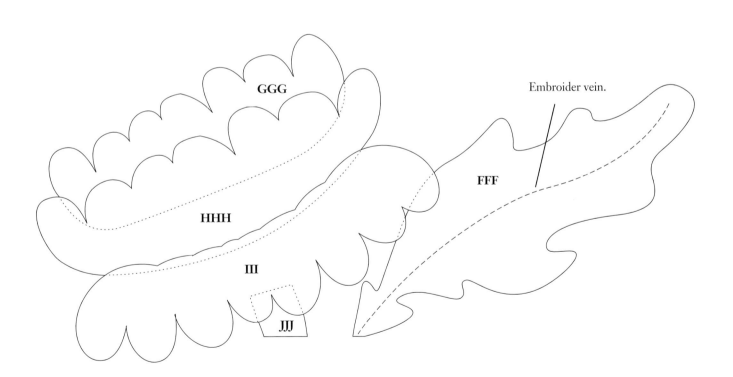

GGG

Embroider vein.

FFF

HHH

III

JJJ

Placement Guide: Chrysanthemum

December
Poinsettia

The red petals of this holiday beauty aren't flowers at all, but simply red leaves. The tiny yellow centers of the plant are actually the flowers.

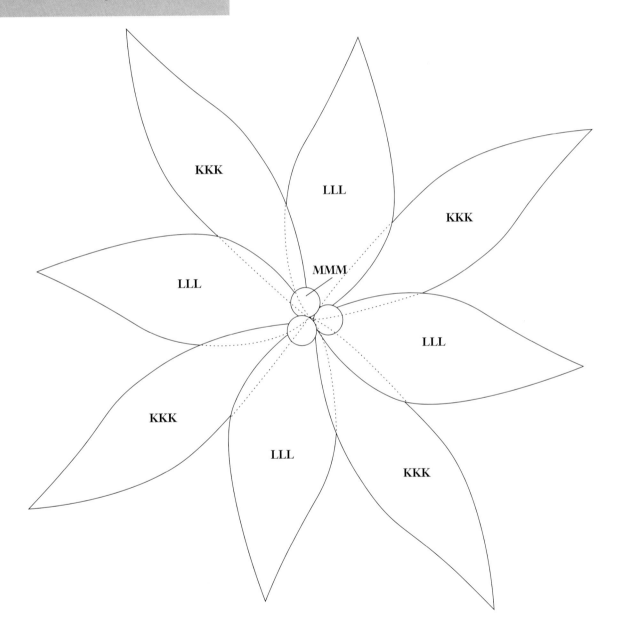

Placement Guide: Poinsettia

Quilt Top Assembly and Finishing

1. From green print, cut 31 (3½" x 12½") sashing strips. From gold print, cut 20 (3½") sashing squares.

2. Referring to **Quilt Top Assembly Diagram**, join 5 sashing strips and 4 blocks as shown to make 1 horizontal row. Repeat to make 2 more horizontal rows.

3. Referring to **Quilt Top Assembly Diagram**, join 4 sashing strips and 5 sashing squares as shown to make 1 sashing row. Repeat to make 3 more sashing rows. Join sashing rows to block rows.

4. From red print, cut 6 (2"-wide) crosswise strips. Cut strips as needed and join end-to-end to make 2 (54"-long) inner borders for sides and 2 (69"-long) inner borders for top and bottom.

5. From pink floral 1, cut 1 (24") square and set aside for binding. From remainder, cut 4 (5"-wide)

lengthwise strips. Cut strips as needed and join end-to-end to make 2 (62"-long) outer borders for sides and 2 (77"-long) outer borders for top and bottom.

6. Matching centers, sew 1 inner border to each outer border. Join borders to quilt top, mitering corners. Press seam allowances toward borders.

7. Layer backing, batting, and quilt top. Baste. Quilt in-the-ditch around flowers and foliage. Quilt cross-hatch pattern approximately 1½" apart in background of blocks. Quilt **Cable Quilting Pattern** in sashing. Quilt **Swag Quilting Pattern** in outer borders.

8. Referring to instructions on page 11, make 8 yards of 2"-wide bias or straight-grain binding from pink floral I. Apply binding to edges of quilt.

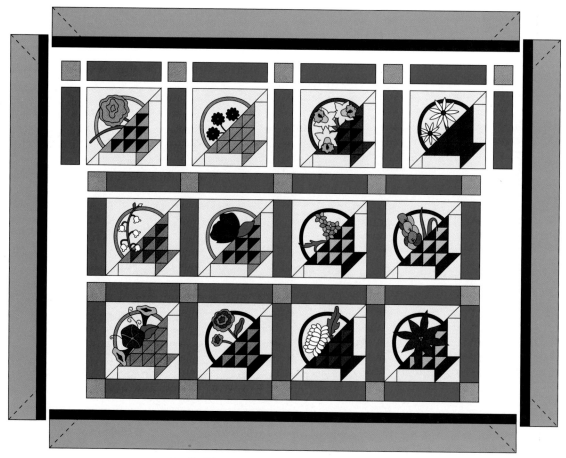

Quilt Top Assembly Diagram

Template Patterns

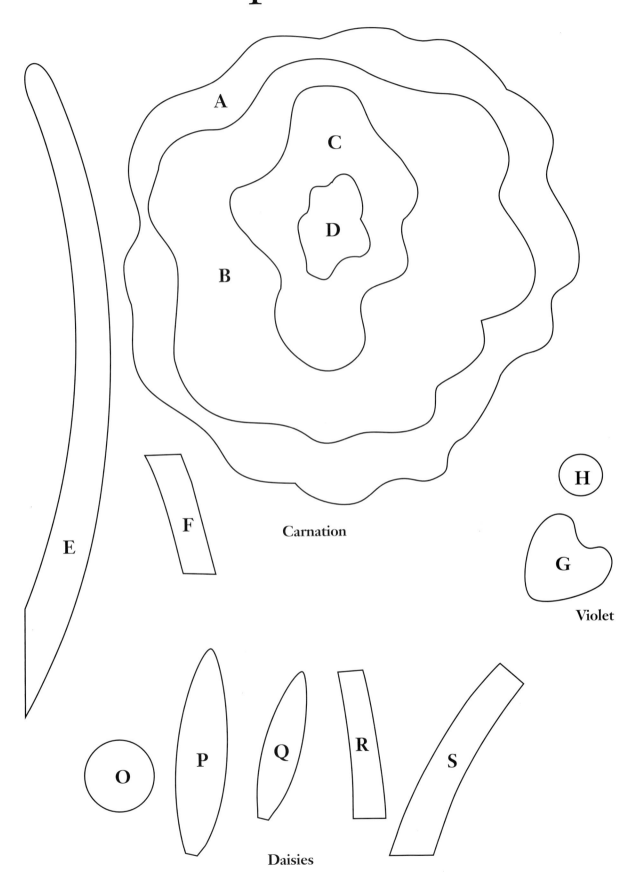

A

C

D

B

E

F

Carnation

H

G

Violet

O

P

Q

R

S

Daisies

41

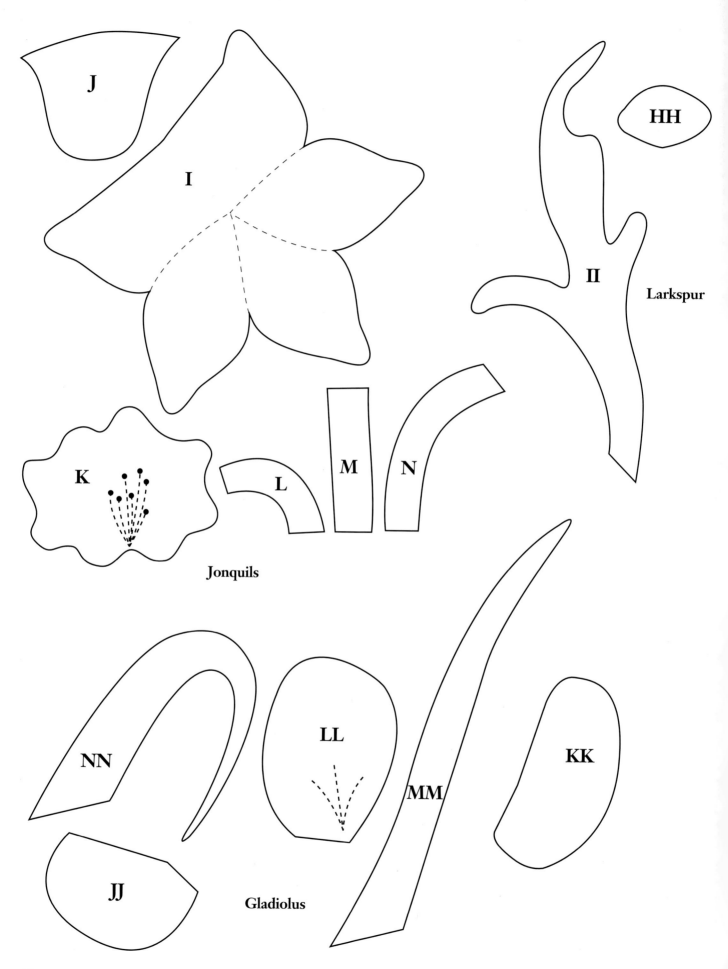

J

I

HH

II

Larkspur

K

L

M

N

Jonquils

NN

LL

MM

KK

JJ

Gladiolus

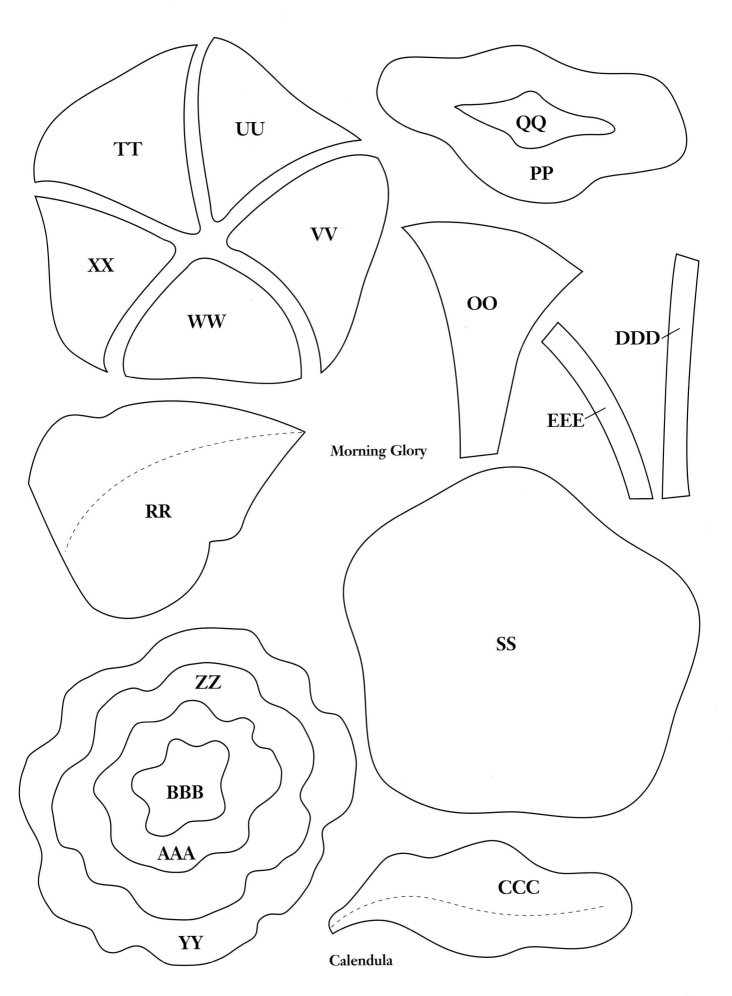

TT

UU

QQ

PP

VV

XX

OO

DDD

WW

Morning Glory

EEE

RR

SS

ZZ

BBB

AAA

CCC

YY

Calendula

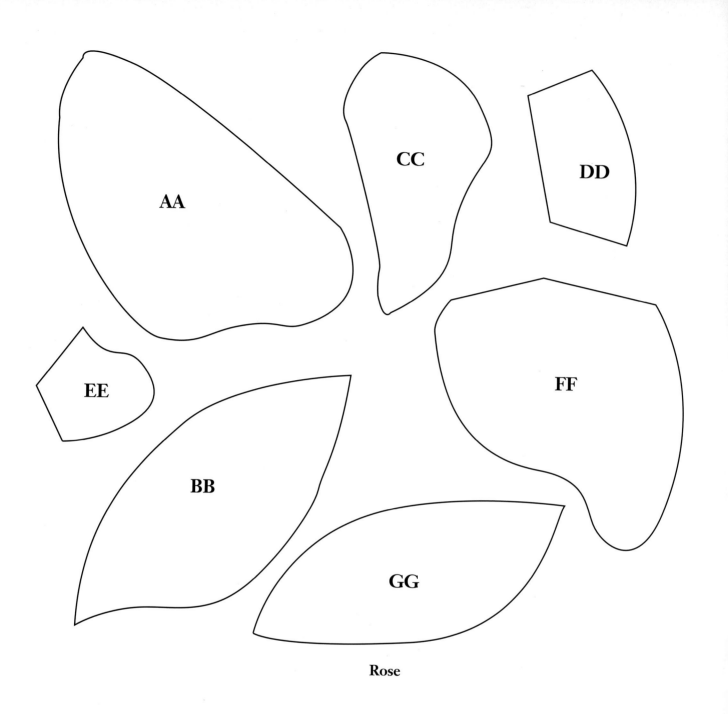

AA

CC

DD

EE

BB

FF

GG

Rose

Poinsettia

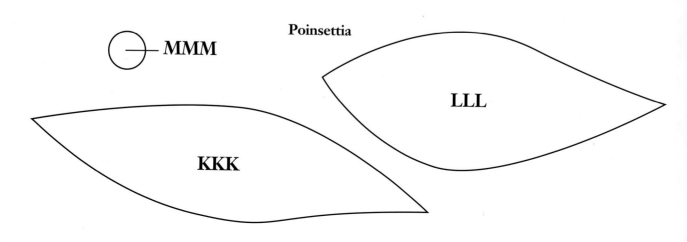

MMM

LLL

KKK

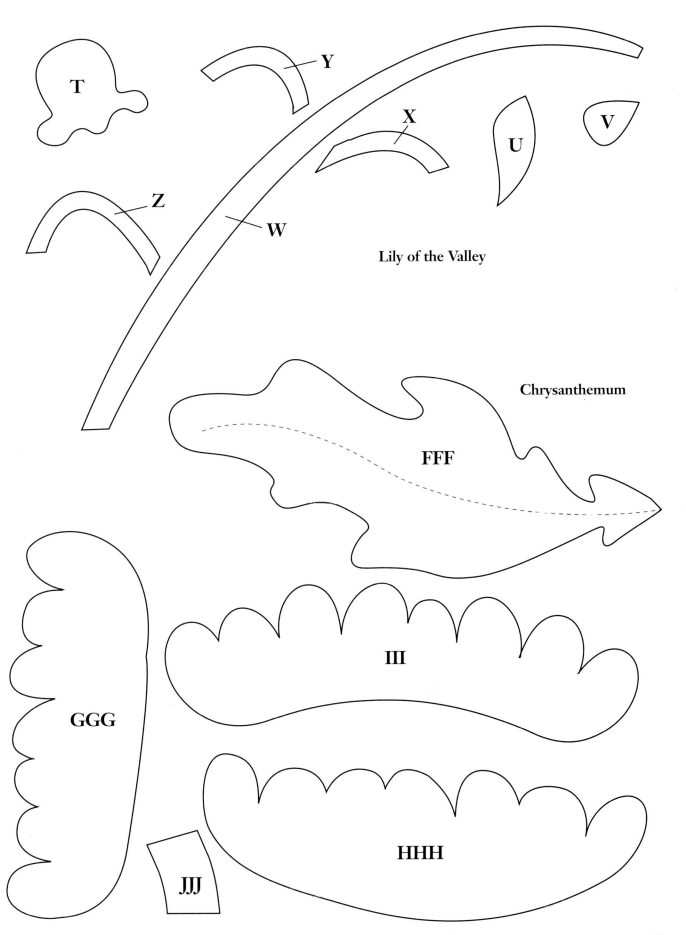

T

Y

X

U

V

Z

W

Lily of the Valley

Chrysanthemum

FFF

III

GGG

HHH

JJJ

45

Quilting Patterns

Swag Pattern Placement Diagram

Cable Quilting Pattern

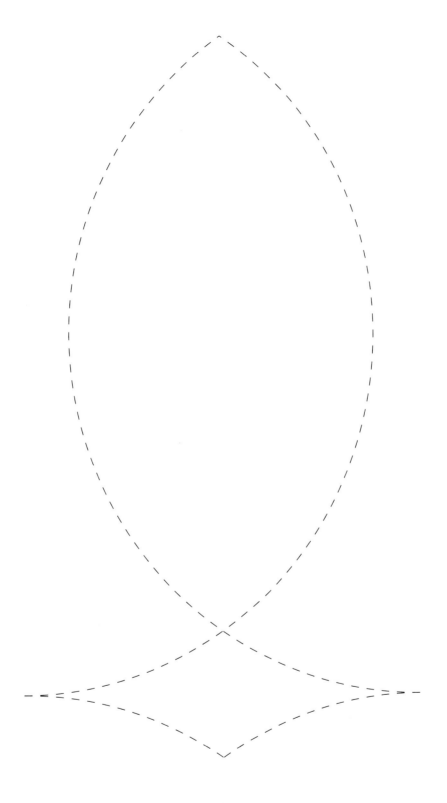

Swag Quilting Pattern

Glossary of Quilting Terms

Acid-free. Tissue paper or boxes that are made without chemicals that can damage fabric over time. Available at art supply stores.

Appliqué. From the French word *appliquer*, meaning "to lay on." Used as a verb to refer to the process of sewing fabric pieces onto a background. Used as a noun to refer to the piece that is sewn onto the background fabric.

Backing. The bottom layer of a finished quilt.

Batting. A soft filling between patchwork top and backing.

Bearding. Migration of loose batting fibers through the quilt top or backing.

Between. A short, small-eyed needle used for quilting. Available in several sizes, indicated by numbers; the higher the number, the shorter the needle.

Bias. The diagonal of a woven fabric, which runs at a 45° angle to the selvage. This is the direction that has the most stretch, making it ideal for curving appliqué shapes and for binding curved edges.

Bicyle clips. Metal or plastic bands designed to hold a cyclist's trousers close to the ankle while riding. Quilters use these clips to secure a rolled quilt during machine quilting.

Binding. A narrow strip of folded fabric that covers the raw edges of a quilt after it is quilted.

Bleeding. The run-off of dye when fabric is wet.

Chain piecing. Machine sewing in which units are sewn one after the other without lifting the presser foot or cutting the thread between units. Also called assembly-line piecing.

Charm quilt. A quilt composed of one shape in many fabrics. Traditionally, no two pieces are cut from the same fabric.

Cross-hatching. Lines of quilting that form a grid of squares or diamonds.

Diagonal corners. A quick-piecing technique that results in a contrasting triangle sewn to one or more corners of a square or rectangle. See page 33 for instructions. Also known as snowball corners.

Echo quilting. One or more lines of quilting that follow the outline of an appliqué piece, so the quilting repeats, or "echoes," the shape. A single line of echo quilting is called outline quilting.

Fat eighth. A 9" x 22" cut of fabric rather than a standard ⅛ yard (4½" x 45").

Fat quarter. An 18" x 22" cut of fabric rather than a standard ¼ yard (9" x 45").

Four-patch. A block comprising four squares or units, joined in two rows of two squares each.

Fusible web. A material made of fibers that melt when heat is applied. Used to fuse two layers of fabric together.

In-the-ditch. Quilting stitches worked very close to or in the seam line.

Nine-patch. A block comprising nine squares or units, joined in three rows of three squares each.

Outline quilting. A single line of quilting that parallels a seam line, approximately ¼" away.

Pin matching. Using straight pins to align two seams so that they will meet precisely when a seam is stitched.

Prairie points. Triangles made from folded squares of fabric that are sewn into seams to provide a dimensional effect. Most often used as an edging.

Quick piecing. One of several techniques that eliminates some marking and cutting steps.

Quilt top. The upper layer of a quilt sandwich, it can be patchwork, appliquéd, or wholecloth. Quilting designs are marked and stitched on the top.

Quilting hoop. A portable wooden frame, round or oval, used to hold small portions of a quilt taut for quilting. A quilting hoop is deeper than an embroidery hoop to accommodate the thickness of the quilt layers.

Reversed patch. A patchwork piece that is a mirror image of another. To cut a reversed patch, turn the template over (reverse it).

Sashing. Strips of fabric sewn between blocks. Also known as lattice stripping.

Selvage. The finished edge of a woven fabric. More tightly woven than the rest of the fabric, selvage is not used for sewing because it may shrink differently when washed.

Set (Setting). The arrangement of joined blocks.

Sleeve. A fabric casing on the back of a quilt through which a dowel is inserted to hang the quilt on a wall.

Straight grain. The horizontal and vertical threads of a woven fabric. Lengthwise grain runs parallel to the selvage. Cross-grain is perpendicular to the selvage.

String piecing. Randomly-sized scraps of fabric that are joined to make a base material, which is then cut into patchwork pieces. Sometimes worked on a foundation.

Strip piecing. A quick-piecing technique in which strips of different fabrics are joined and then cut into segments that become units of a patchwork block.

Template. A pattern guide, made of sturdy material, that is traced to mark the pattern shape onto fabric.

Triangle-square. A patchwork square that is composed of triangles. When two triangles are joined to make a square, these are called half-square triangles. When four triangles are joined to make a square, these are called quarter-square triangles. Triangles should be cut and sewn so that the straight grain falls on the square's outer edge.